D0597445

A Book of
Blessings, New-birth Stones,
and
New-birth Cries

birthquakes

by

Norman C. Habel

Photographs

by

Lorence G. Collins

Fortress Press   Philadelphia

Library of Congress Catalog Card Number

ISBN 0-8006-0075-4

Designed by Otto Reinhardt

3910G73 Printed in the United States of America 1-75

A COLLECTION OF NEW-BIRTH STONES

Most people think of birthstones as precious gems like emeralds and sapphires. New-birth stones are different. They are like the people whom they portray, people like you and me. We are not exceptional beauties or handsome specimens. We have rough edges and often lack lustre. We are much like the pebbles on the roadside. But hidden within each of us are colors so bright they would dazzle the eye. By a new birth we can be transformed and recreated to display our new colors and new selves. That new birth is possible only through the Light of life, the Light of the world. His penetrating light can change even the most drab rock into a living stone.

The photographs in this book are not a new form of modern art; they are pictures of new-birth stones. That is, they all come from rocks so ordinary and so dull that we would probably have overlooked them or thrown them away. These stones are like the pebbles that you walk on in the street or the backyard. Yet you have never seen their real beauty. Inside they are filled with magic color and the mysteries of creation.

These pictures are photographs of rock sections magnified about one hundred times. The rocks had to be cut with a diamond saw. Each section was ground to one-thousandth of an inch thick and then mounted on a glass slide. This thickness is about one-fourth the thickness of a sheet of paper. At this thickness most minerals are transparent and, when viewed through a microscope, take on interesting shapes and colors. This is particularly true of these sections when seen through polarized light.

The color of these rocks is not released unless they are subjected to violent grinding, and unless a special kind of light vibrates through them. Therein lies the mystery and the parable of these rocks. They are portraits of our new birth. For unless our old selves are stripped away and subjected to the light of Christ, we remain lifeless. Through him we are born again.

There is a stone here for your birthday week, a stone that hides a mystery, a name, and a message. That stone captures the magic of your new birth. For the rock hounds and earth lovers among you, the geological names of these stones have also been indicated.

A BOOK OF BLESSINGS AND BIRTH CRIES

Instead of a happy horoscope or a sign from the stars for the week of your birth, this book offers you blessings and new-birth cries. For the week of your birthday or your baptismal birthday, there is a personal blessing and birth cry. For each week of the year there is a blessing and birth cry to use as you wish. Each blessing is expressed in two ways: as a direct word from my soul to yours and as a compact message drawn from nature and the Scriptures. With each blessing comes a new-birth cry to scream or whisper as you struggle to make the blessing come true in your life.

A blessing is a power. The power comes from deep within and reaches deep into someone else. Blessings are not passing thoughts or quick messages. Blessings are deep words to live with, to dwell on, to grow by. They are part of someone else given for you to treasure. They come from the Christ in me and reach out to the hope in you. They are part of my life power that longs to stir your spirit.

When men like Abraham or Jacob were about to die they passed on their blessing to their sons. Those blessings were filled with sacred power and holy magic. They could not be changed once they were spoken. They expressed the very character of the person blessed. Some of the inner self, the deep soul of the old man, was transferred to his children. Their destiny was wrapped up in his words. Those words opened up a future for them. The blessing they received was a promise, and with the promise was imparted the power to fulfill the promise.

When Jacob wrestled in the night with an angel of God he received a blessing. As the dawn broke he pinned the angel down and cried, "I will not let you go until you bless me." Jacob won his blessing, the power for a new life. His blessing was a new name, the name Israel. With that new name came a new identity, a new meaning to life, a new character, a new man.

Jacob's blessing did not come without a struggle. He was not born anew without the agony of birth pangs, without a long night of wrestling with God. He cried out for God's blessing and would not let God go until it had been received. Similar cries are offered in this book. They are the cries of people struggling with God and straining to become who they really are in Christ. They are the birth pangs of those who yearn to be born anew or who long to be true to their new selves. They are the birthquakes of those becoming free, birthquakes that shake old lives and old worlds.

By the way, you will feel the impact of these birthquakes even more if you read the Old Testament passages given for each week.

A YEAR OF WORSHIP IDEAS

The blessings and birth cries in this book are also a series of themes and thoughts for worship. Their starting point is the given set of Old Testament texts which begin with creation and trace the creative deeds of God through from the beginning of all things to the coming of Christ.

Creation themes are central in this book. Various elements of creation, like the stars, the wind, or fire, are selected as primary biblical images or realities that are used to convey the blessings. These images are also expressed in the corresponding rock pictures. It is not merely that we are using nature as an analogy to express our faith. Nature also worships with us. Creation yearns with us for its own liberation and ours. This book invites you to spend a year of worship with nature, to dwell on the bond we have with creation, and to observe how God moves through the works of creation to reveal his splendor.

Linked with creation is the theme of new birth and new life in Christ. Life in Christ involves reliving our new birth whenever we retreat to the warmth of the womb. That process evokes new birth pangs and cries of joy. Life in Christ is life in a different dimension, an eternal dimension that is very much a part of reality. We who are in Christ are part of a new order of creation, a new life within life. That dimension of life we have called the seventh dimension. We invite you to worship aware of that new dimension and alive to that new reality.

The rock pictures are also available in filmstrip form, where they are even more exotic than the reproductions in this book. An accompanying record is also available on which the message of the numbered blessings is dramatically reinforced in sound and music. Those who wish to adapt these materials in connection with their church worship program will find in the rear of this book a table which correlates the Birthquake themes and prayers with the Sundays and festival days of the church year.

birthquakes

january 1-7   your blessing is a wind flame that pierces the empty night
and enters your searching soul to give you life blazing true

wind

psalm 104:1-4

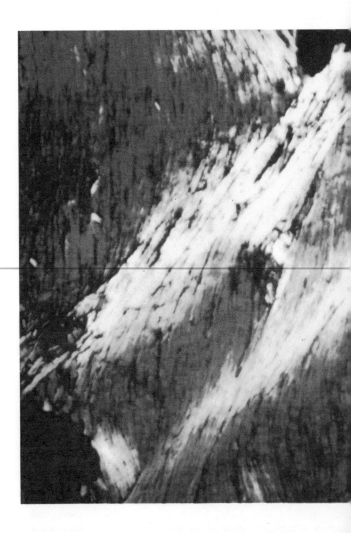

*In the beginning is the wind flame.
And the wind flame is God. The wind
flame penetrates the emptiness and
life begins to be.*

Flame

chlorite schist

God of gods
and Flame of flames,
spin,
spin through my emptiness
and wrap me in flames
as once you clothed
the birth
of life itself
long, long ago
in the deep void.

Wind Flame of life,
whirl, whirl through my cold world,
and make me alive to life,
life by Flame,
life in a new dimension,
life in a seventh dimension.

Wind Flame of birth,
breathe,
breathe in the void of my soul
a new human me,
that is truly human,
truly free
and truly me.

Wind Flame of song,
plunge,
plunge through my fears
and bring me to birth
as a new being
with a new beginning
and a new song of courage.

Come Christ,
burst into flesh
and create in me
a new me
wrapped in flame
and trembling with birthquakes.

january 8-14   your blessing is a magic deep whose dark glistening waters tremble beneath the wind breath that stirs your birth from the deep

magic deep

genesis 1:1-2

2 *In the beginning the world lies dor-
mant in the deep. And the deep is
magic, quivering at the brink of birth
beneath the hovering wind flame of
God.*

From the beginning, Lord,
deep calls to deep
and the magic black quivers,
quivers
in the sleeping world womb.

From the beginning, Lord,
the deep calls to me,
calls me back
to be born.

The dream of the deep
is magic
with fascination of what might be,
with wonder at what will be,
with wisdom at what must be.

The deep calls to my deep
to return to the womb
and be born a second time.

The deep
calls me to tremble
beneath the flame breath
and burst forth from the water
a new human, a true human.

Lord Jesus,
you roared forth victorious
from the deep
to recreate this world from within.
Birth me again and again
into being me,
birth me from the waters
deep with Spirit
and with hope.

Make me so human it hurts
and make me a part of that life
which is deeper
than death.

bubbles in Canada balsam cement

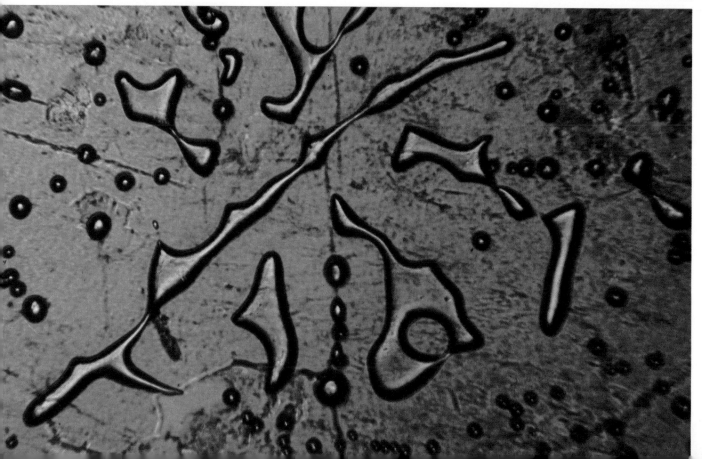

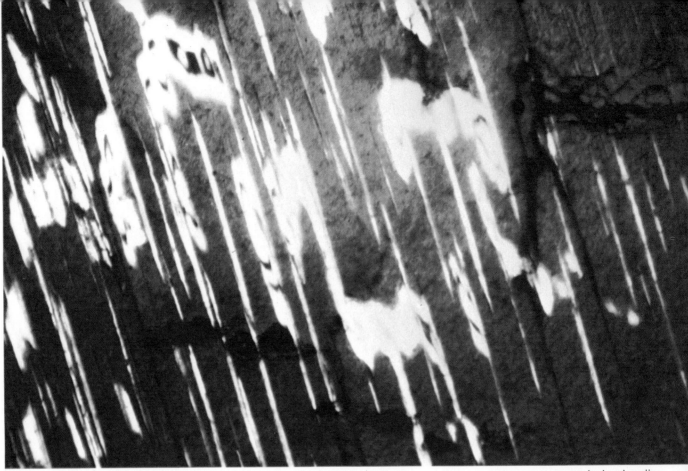

muscovite in microcline

january 15-21   your blessing is a lightning word that splits the silent night
                  of your agony and stirs a new you dormant in your deep

genesis 1:3-5

The first word in the night is light.
The light is a lightning word that
strikes the groaning deep with bolts of
blazing life.

Lightning Word

Word,
wonder word from nowhere,
roll on down,
thunder on through,
and rumble across the deep night.

Word,
lightning word from the night,
flash your fire,
flash your life
across the dark womb of the deep.

Word,
light word trom the womb,
echo on down,

spiral on through
the caverns of chaos
and the tunnels of history
. . . to us.

Word,
life word from the past,
break through,
crash through from death to life
from the dead of night,
to announce a banquet of being
and the birth of love.

Strike us
with your lightning word

and break the surface of our lives
that we might know love.

Help us experience love
by passing from death to life
for someone in pain.
Help us learn love
by living with someone
from tomb to self-awakening
. . . his and ours.

Come Christ, our lightning word,
and crack our lives wide open
for loving
at the deeps of living.

january 22-28   your blessing is a butterfly sky where you can fly risen from your
old crippling cocoon into the soaring freedom of the heavens

genesis 1:6-8

4 *Sweeping through the deep, God pitches heaven on high. The high of heaven is a glittering butterfly sky where Lazarus laughs with the risen Lord and invites us all to fly with him.*

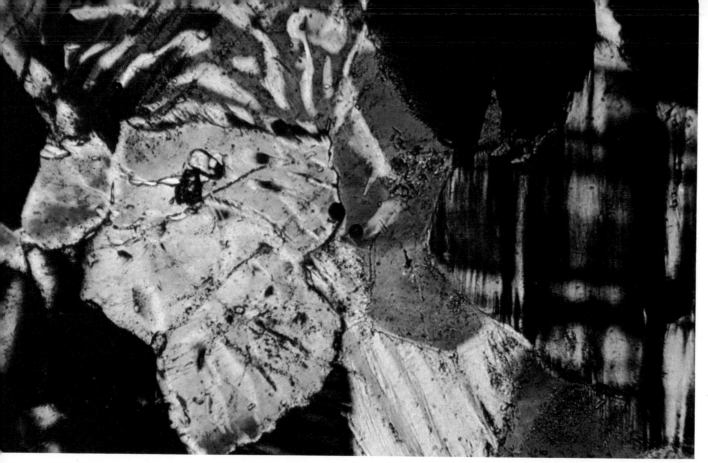

myrmekite

butterfly sky

Lord,
you called the firmament heaven,
a cosmic cocoon
for holding back the great sky waters
that rumble like a mountain waterfall.

You fixed a gulf
between heaven and hell
so that no one can cross,
no one with a drop of moisture
from the waterfall above,
no one,
no one but the butterflies.

For us the butterflies come
washed in dew,
aflame with royal colors
and bright with messages
from the blue.

Help us to see them, Lord,
as messengers of your love,
your first love for us.

Tell your love story
deep in our hearts and minds,
the story of your only Son

crossing the chasm from death
to give us true life,
risen life,
life in a new dimension.

Give us your love through him,
a love that casts out fear,
the fear of being nothing
and dying alone.
Free us to love,
to be who we are
and enjoy the butterfly sky
where Lazarus laughs.

your blessing is a morning star chorus celebrating the birth pangs of
earth where you are torn from the soil to sing their hallelujahs of birth

job 38:1-7

For us, Lord,
the morning stars sing
to celebrate the dawn,
just as on that first fresh day
when every glowing galaxy was new
the stars spun wild
and sang
of the new-found earth below.

For us, Lord,
there is pain in finding,
in being found,
in admitting we are lost
light years
from where we thought we were,
love years
from who we thought we were.

When we return
and trace our path through falls
to our very own beginning,
we are humbled
and small
and hidden in shells.

Find us, Lord.
Be as near
as those who have found themselves
and now are found in you.
Give them the love
to help us find ourselves.

Find us
in our suffering,
in their suffering,
in the suffering of Christ for us.

Then let there be joy in heaven,
a morning star chorus.
Let us discover
your mystery on earth . . .
our very own selves.

5

*In the dawn the morning stars explode
with song. There is joy in heaven over
the latest gift of God. The world is
ready to be unwrapped, the earth is
being born.*

Morning Star Chorus

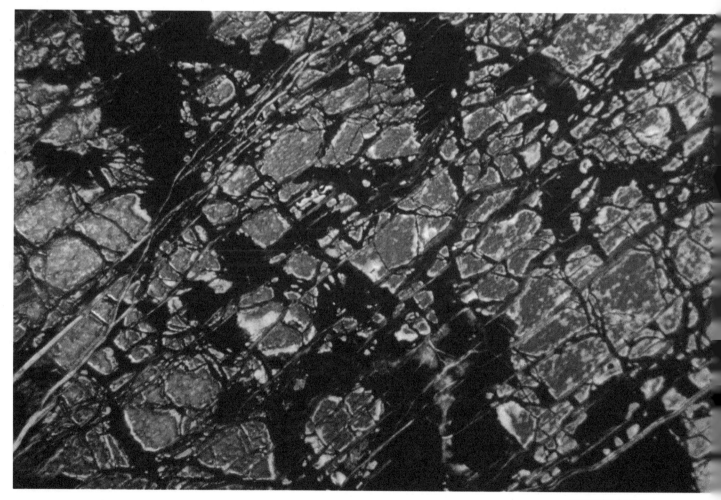

serpentized olivine

muscovite-quartz schist

february 5-11   your blessings are silent birthquakes that convulse your soul
to signal a new birth from your tomb of inner desperation

silent birthquakes

For us, Lord,
the earth was born warm
when the first peak
burst through the cosmic womb,
the swollen waters of chaos,
and felt the touch of life,
the life rays of God.

Now that ancient earth groans
with birthquakes,
birth pangs of yearning
for a new world
free from the bondage of death,
free from the rape of nature
by violent children.

The earth quakes in travail,
in secret birth,
that we too might be born free,
that our dying might be birth,
that our agony might be a sign,
a whisper of the new world,
a thrust of liberation.

The new world has been stirring
since you rose, Lord,
and sent tremors of new life
vibrating abroad
from your shattered tomb.

New rhythms,
new selves,
and new worlds
are already growing
within this groaning universe.

Make us
a vital part of their birth.
Make the new being in us
the living clue
that the new order of Christ
is now coming to be
in us
through silent birthquakes.

genesis 1:9-13

6

With cosmic birth come birthquakes.
The deep rumbles in travail as the
earth emerges to light. The earth in
turn yearns with birthquakes awaiting
the birth of human lives.

your blessing is an ocean stampede now tamed for you to ride victorious through the universe and triumphant through your death

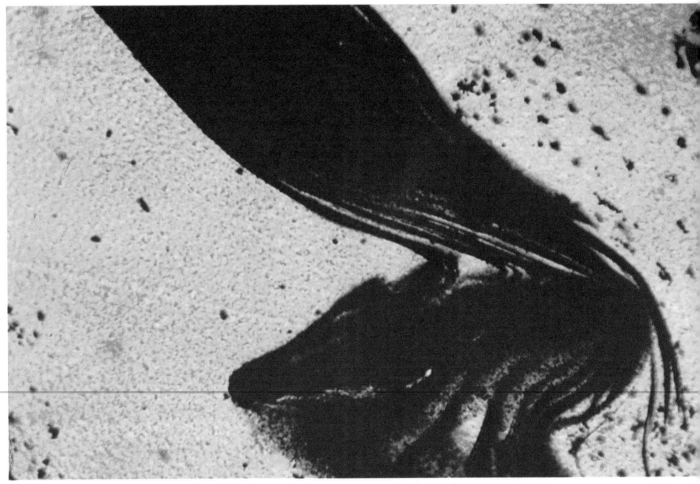

obsidian

7 *From the deep, chaos erupts like a
raging dragon, an ocean stampede.
God roars in to tame this chaos beast
and ride his dragon sidesaddle into the
sunset . . . laughing all the way.*

There goes Leviathan, Lord,
that clumsy old dragon
thrashing the ocean face.
He roams with the memory
of the great stampede
when the untamed ocean
stormed the earth
with fuming flood and fury.

From your sky high boat
you muzzled that old dragon.
You penned in the ocean with beaches
where now we're free to play
and watch you ride Leviathan
across the red horizon.

Does Leviathan live only
in the deeps of the sea, Lord?

Wherever you call us to fish
Leviathan lurks
and threatens chaos.
The smoldering spirit of stampede
still rises like an ogre in the night.

Lord of the ocean,
you were crushed in one stampede
of devils, death, and demons.
But you rose triumphant
from chaos,
from depths lower than hell.

Now you call us to fish
in this wild human stampede,
this turmoil of evil.

Well, give us a dragon to ride,
a harpoon from heaven,
and the courage to laugh at Leviathan.

Then we'll be fishers of men.

psalm 104:24-30

Stampede

february 19-25   your blessing is a whirlwind clay that dances forth
from the brittle dust, alive and you and truly human

genesis 2:4-8

8 *Silent in the desert dawn a Sculptor
molds his whirlwind clay. His breath,
like wind flame, enters the cold clay
and living figures dance forth from the
dust of death.*

whirlwind clay

Like a potter, Lord,
your gentle fingers
pressed the clay into a mold,
a smooth human shape.

You liked it
and wanted it to live with you
in your desert garden.
You embraced the clay
and mouth to mouth
you breathed a spirit in the clay,
a deep whirlwind whisper.

What once was buried in dust
arose to live,

to be a human being
with the print of the potter
fresh in the clay.

Make me alive to that same spirit,
to the whirlwind clay
you created me to be.

Let me rise from the dust
afresh
and aware
of what it means to be.

Come, Christ,
human being unlimited.

You roared from the dust
like a whirlwind from death
leaping ashes,
rattling lives,
and rocking the gates of hell
to liberate men of clay.

Liberate me today.
Cause the same upheaval in me
that transforms earth
into birth,
and lifeless dust
into vibrant human beings
as free as you, Christ,
as free as you!

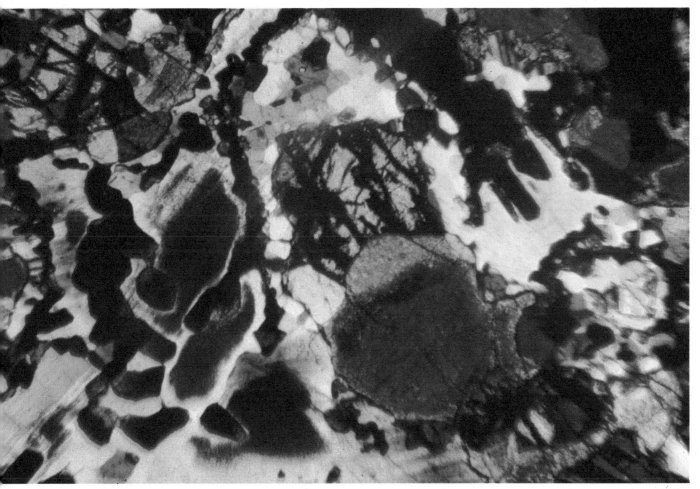

meta-gabbro

february 26-march 4

your blessing is a suffering tree where you can carve your name in the pain of faith to live forever new and forever you

genesis 2:9-17

9 *On earth there is a garden with two trees of expectation, the splendor tree and the suffering tree. We choose the first and leave the garden. God offers the second in the shape of a cross.*

suffering tree

pyroxene amphibolite

In the cool of the garden, Lord,
two trees still grow
reaching for the sun.

The first is glistening green,
alive with fireworks
and bursting with lights.
It promises to splash my name
across the neon sky
and hail me
as the one the world should notice
and the one whom God will praise.

The wages are life
and I get my name in lights
for everyone to see . . . for a while.

The other tree is charred,
wrinkled and torn.
It's a listening tree,
a suffering tree
deep in the garden of God.

Lead me there, Lord,
I've lost my name in lights,
in the fast fling of life.

Let me see the tree of Eden
grow again at the center of earth
. . . in the shape of a cross.

Carve my name there.
Let me grow into the tree,
grow into new life,
grow into freedom
through your death on that tree.

Make that tree my freedom tree,
the center of my life,
the sign of who I am
growing free
. . . through suffering with you.

your blessing is an Eden sunset inviting you back through molten gates to a new freedom under the apple tree

plagioclase

genesis 3:1-13

10

Outside the garden gates we watch the sun set red on Eden's trees. Our Father's call lingers in the sunset of his anger: "Man, where are you? Return through the molten gates to freedom. The apples are ripe now."

Eden Sunset

For us the sun sets red
through the tall trees of Eden.
It hovers high
with flames of glory
inviting us back past the fire
to you, our Father.

Your soft haunting voice
still rings through the orchard
with the words,
"Where are you?
Where are you, children?
Adam? Eve?"

A simmering voice within us
urges us to cry,
"We're coming, Father.
We're coming."

But the gates of Eden
are molten red
and the sun sets in anger.

One man broke the barrier,
one man rent the anger,
one man,
our Brother from the deep.

Walk with us, Lord Jesus,
through those molten gates,
through the sun that hides our Father,
through the fire that kills the flesh
and makes us human,
the sons and daughters of tomorrow
and true children of our Father.

Lord Jesus, is it true
our Father has a plan
to turn old Eden into city parks
and to bring us back again,
fireproofed for living
through the heat and anger
of the city
where freedom is born?

march 12-18   your blessing is a desert fox racing forgiven across the
shifting sands and protected for new life with you

genesis 4:1-15

|| *Beyond the gates of God we run like
Cain. We are desert foxes trying to live
by cunning instead of concern, by
looting instead of liberation.*

desert

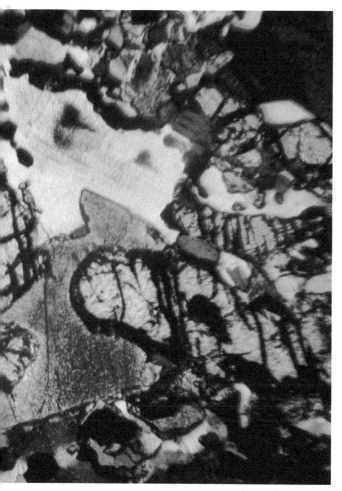

hypersthene gabbro

Fox

Lord, the desert fox
is now protected
from the fervor of the hunters
and the terror of their traps.

He is free
to roam the sands at will,
a forgiven murderer
redeemed by God.

As such he is a cousin to Cain
and my brother,
a creature with a mark of grace.

I too bear the scars
of dodging through the desert
where serpent fangs
and friendly hunters
prevent me finding joy
in what I am.

It seems sometimes
I die of thirst
and bleak loneliness.

Then you come with mercy
to forgive my past misdeeds
and I survive.

Come now, Lord of life!
You died in the desert for me
to be free.
Let me live anew
not merely by the old cunning I knew
but by the cunning of Christ
called grace.

Give me that mark of grace
to show the world
that Christ the Victor takes my side
and that I will never die
no matter what oppressors say.

I may even lose my tail
but I'll never lose my life.

your blessing is Enoch Rock, the earth rock given for treasures, for taking dangerous walks through life and making all things green

enoch rock

genesis 4:17-26

12 *We are given a rock on which to run with grace and take our walks with God. Our rock is the very ground that Enoch trod.*

perthite

For us, Lord,
the underworld surrendered,
the rocks gave up their secrets,
their copper and gold,
their hidden veins of magic ore.

They gave themselves to Enoch
and he built a city,
a sleek civilization.
To his sons they gave their souls.

Old Enoch went with God
on long walks.

He had the image of God,
the mind of God
to keep the rock green.

Now we all want a sample,
a piece of Enoch Rock,
the inexhaustible earth
that gives birth to men and music.

Then you came, Lord,
a Son of Enoch on long walks
across the rock
and down the lanes of Palestine.

You carried the image of God,
a mind to change people
from abusing themselves,
their neighbors,
and their world.

You came to save the rock
by dying in its heart
and calling us to love the rock
with tubas, tulips, and tears.
Walk through the world with us, Lord,
and teach us to tend the rock.

march 26-april 1   your blessing is a flood bird soaring high from the under-
water caverns of deep death to your new world of birth

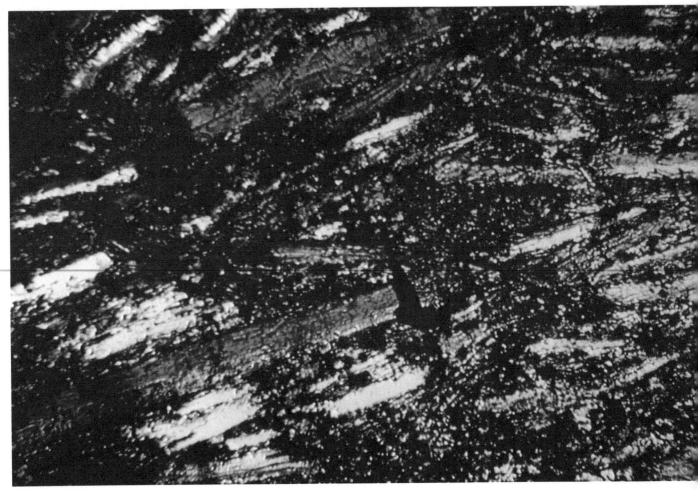

trachyte

genesis 8:1-13

13 *Across the rock, floods sweep deep with death. We lie trapped in our caverns unless God gives us the soul of a flood bird. Flood birds have the faith to writhe and soar from death to a new life high above the flood.*

Lord of the sky,
I sometimes feel like a bird
caught in a cave.
I am a swallow about to drown,
a dove trapped in the deep,
a little bird.

The floods cover the earth
and crowd life into corners
too tight for me to be me.

Free me!
Free me
with the grace you gave Noah.

Enter me, Christ, with a song,
with the faith to plunge upward,
with the courage
to face the storms of the deep
and rise.

Let me strain for the sky.
Fling me out of my cave
into the deep
until I circle up
up
up through the waters,
up to the surface,
up to the sky.

Rise with me
until I see you risen,
dancing with Noah and the animals
in the mountain meadows of Ararat.

Let me be untimely born,
newborn,
a flood bird free,
scanning the wet clay of earth
where men are made
of water and the wind.

Free me, Lord,
to fly over the flood.

Flood bird

your blessing is a rainbow blast breaking through a thunder sky of
terror to free you for peace on earth and integrity among men

genesis 9:8-17

I see your world, Lord,
through strange filters,
through curtains of sound and color
that seem to hide your eyes,
your fire voice,
your glory.

Where are you?

For a moment my nerve ends may tingle
and my senses may be sharp enough
to taste the silence
or hear a rainbow whisper
words of peace
like those that Noah heard.

Then a thick veil covers my dreams
and falls like night on my ears
until I hear nothing
but empty echoes,
fog horns that punctuate the darkness
and jolt my fears with cold spasms.

Rend the veil
that covers my senses,
my soul, and my self.

Strip the film from my eyes,
the coating from my ears.
Dampen the clay with your lips
and touch my ears, my eyes,
and my soul.
Let me see a rainbow
blast through the thunder sky
to free me from my web
and announce peace on earth with power.

14

*Above the fleeing floods a rainbow
breaks through the heaving skies with
a promise of new life, free from
drowning.*

Break through, Jesus Christ,
and free me from every veil
hiding your victory
and mine.

rainbow blast

biotite granite

april 9-15   your blessing is a silly seed once promised Abraham that laughs its way through hard-core history to come alive in you, green and true

amphibolite

genesis 18:1-19

15

The promise falls as a seed, a silly seed from lifeless Abraham. Its silly grin is the sign of life by promise, life in a new dimension.

Abraham must have looked silly, Lord,
leaning on his walking stick
and talking to the sky.
He thought he heard a promise
that his seed would be as the stars
and that he would one day
give his inner life
to revive the lives of others.

At high noon in the desert
a dusty stranger came
to eat his best food
and tell him a joke
about old old Sarah having a son
and giving him seed.

That's silly, Lord.

No wonder Sarah laughed,
and Abraham laughed, and the camels laughed
. . . until the promise came true
and they called their son "Laughter."

Teach me to laugh, Lord,
when believing you seems silly,
when living by promises instead of proofs
seems childish and pointless,
when trusting my friends or you
to change my life
is like living a big joke.

How can I live by your promise
of what can be
instead of proofs of what will be?

Give me the faith of one mustard seed,
one silly mustard seed,
that can grow in the crevice of rocks.
Teach me to laugh when they ask for proof
that my inner life is a seed sown long ago.
Assure me that I am a son of Abraham
raised from the stones by Jesus Christ,
the firstfruit of seeds asleep.

your blessing is a flame tree blazing holy and summoning you to find your new self purged by bitter fire

Lord, where can I find,
something so sacred today,
an altar so holy,
a mountain so mysterious
that no one will touch it?

Have we lost the hidden power
of holy places?

Where can I feel the holy,
the magic fire that glows
deep in the heart of things
that you have touched?

exodus 3:1-12

When Moses reached the mystery mountain
you came in flame.
Old Moses had to shed his shoes
to walk the holy ground,
the red hot earth
around that flame tree.

Will you lead me to a flame tree,
to a burning place so sacred,
a moment so holy
I can feel the touch of fire
purging my spirit?

Will you put a burning coal to my lips
and my life
to cleanse me of my leprosy,
or crucify my flesh on a tree,
the untouchable flame tree
where you suffered hell?

Make me into holy ground,
human clay
alive to mystery
and free to free my friends.
Fill me, Christ, with your spirit,
your holy wind,
and then perhaps I will see you
leap in flames
from the trees in my yard.

16

*The promise is ratified by fire. Moses
walks on holy ground and a flame tree
calls him to liberate his fellows by
fire.*

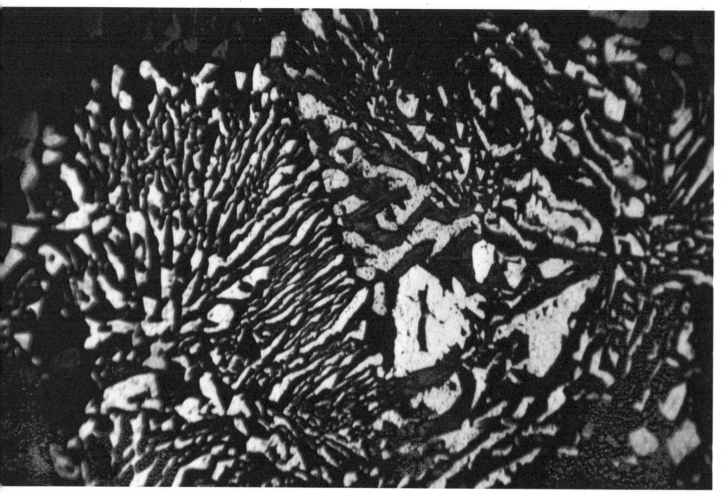

micropegmatite

your blessing is a freedom bread to be eaten with suffering among the oppressed who long for true justice . . . from you

zoned pyroxene in volcanic porphyry

freedom bread

exodus 12:21-32

17 *The promise of freedom ferments in the chains of oppression. God's people eat their freedom bread with rage. Their rice is a sacrament of revolution and their God a suffering brother.*

Lord, the long night is bitter
when masters old and new
strive to rule my soul.
They all promise freedom
but they give me bondage,
a place beside the Israelites
treading mud for bricks
that others own.

In the long night
I long for a dangerous dawn
when my soul is my own,
sold to no one,
no matter how kind.

The night is longest
when death lurks at the door
rattling my shutters.

Are you there
when I eat freedom bread with friends,
the sacrament of revolution,
remembering the Israelites
and all who live in chains
of body, soul, and mind?

The sympathy of suffering is good,
but I look for more.

Come, Christ,
and help me find true freedom,
not escape or empathy,
not a wild escapade along the seashore
running naked through the night
after silver gulls.

Give me the spirit to stand alone
against all grand masters
and never doubt my stand,
never doubt who I am,
never be someone else's fool.

Be my freedom bread, Lord,
my freedom rice,
my life.

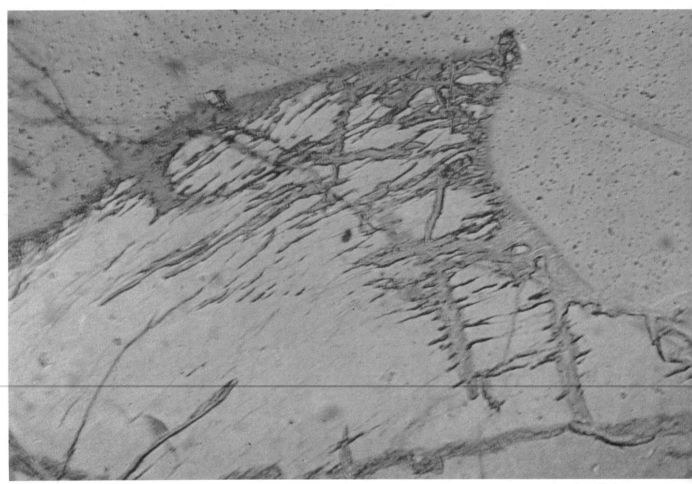

altered cordierite

tidal sweep

your blessing is a tidal sweep on the day of your liberation, your exodus through the raging waters of death, disgrace, and ugly insecurity

exodus 14:19-31

We're ready for the ride, Lord,
the tidal sweep
of full liberation.

We're ready for the tall waves,
the roaring waters of the Red Sea,
hurricane blasts from heaven
and your own red tornado cloud
hovering on the horizon.

We're ready for an exodus,
for the rocks of revolution
and the tidal waters
of a new baptism.

We're ready to break with Egypt,
with every ugly oppression on earth,
and rise from the river
shouting, Hallelujah.

We're ready
but we're very very scared.

The earthquakes have begun,
the birthquakes are growing,
the tidal wave is rising . . .
and our faith is failing.

What will tomorrow be like?

Lord, you liberated Israel,
you broke from the grave
and rode the waves to victory.
Be with us now
as this new age invades.
Lead us through this tidal sweep
to a new day
when lives are baptized with your Spirit.

Make it an age
when freedom is born
from the depths of your love
by the healing hands of your Son.

18

The birthquakes grow with intensity as we pass through the roaring deep on the exodus road to freedom. The tidal sweep of liberation rises like the waters of the Red Sea.

may 7-13   your blessing is a mountain magic shimmering from the glory
cloud that calls you to covenant your life and climb by promise

plagioclase phenocryst in volcanic porphyry

exodus 19:1-9

19   *Those who taste freedom have a
mountain magic waiting, a glimpse of
the wind flame on high. Freedom
means covenant, trust, and the promise to learn who we are.*

mountain magic

Where is the mountain magic,
the mystery of Mount Sinai
that lures and laughs,
frightens and fascinates?

Where is the magic of the cloud
that radiated fire
and hypnotized Moses?

Where is the spirit of a Moses
who could mediate a covenant
between a God of fire
and a hard-nosed people?

Where is the magic of Jesus,
the man who healed on holy days
and made secure souls shudder?
Where is the mystery of his mountain
where he talked with Moses
until everything glowed with glory?

Has the magic gone underground,
invisible to sceptical spectators
who lack the inner eyes
to see the flame of the Father
above all and in all
and through all?

Arouse in me the faith
to see the flame world,
the new world of Christ
moving mysteriously behind the scenes,
behind the routine,
behind the news.

Make me alive to the rhythm
of Christ
changing me and my Father's world.
Make me a priest
touched by your mountain magic.

your blessing is a molten thunder erupting in deep volcanos to announce your resurrection from the prisons of cruel conformity

exodus 19:10-20

Lord,
your volcanos are violent gifts
that breathe forth anger
from the deep of earth
where rock is born.

When your holy voice gets to me
and exposes my hidden idols,
my ugly acts toward others,
then my conscience quivers
and I feel the anger rising from below.

It's as though old Sinai
erupts again
and flings in my face
those two tablets of law
that Moses etched in fresh hot stone.

I feel like a naughty child
trying to escape
the violence deep within me.

Don't let me run.

Take me to the center of earth,
the core of the law,
the eye of the volcano
where you erupted with molten thunder
breaking the grip of death
and freeing men from the law.

New life was born with you,
a volcanic birth
from the land of death.

Give me that new life
as you forgive me my past.
Keep me free from frightened people
who try to mold your molten word
into lifeless stone walls.

Teach me to leap walls
and rise daily from old volcanos.

20

The free hear a molten thunder erupting from God's mountain and walk the lava way by faith. For the insecure the lava thunder spells terror and torment.

altered pyroxene amphibolite

molten thunder

may 21-27

your blessing is a summit banquet where you are invited to commune in the sky and celebrate your new creation from the pieces of your broken past

exodus 24:1-11

Lord of the banquet,
I long
to partake of your body and blood,
to join with your people,
with those who know the new life.

I come to eat a summit meal with them,
to celebrate the mystery
of the new dimension to life
that invaded earth
when you rose from the grave.

Why then do I feel somber
when I come to your table?
Why don't I experience
an exciting communion with God
like those who dined on Sinai
and beheld his splendor?

Somehow
the old me never dies.

Cast it out, Lord!
Let my new life return,
let my new nature show through,
let the new me be.

Make my next communion truly holy,
a summit banquet of new life,
a celebration of the mystery
that the risen Christ now rules
in, with, and under our world.

His rule
is the seventh dimension of life.
Let it be!

Blow the trumpet to celebrate
the next summit banquet
with him.
Blow it hard!

21

The free are invited to a summit banquet with God in his glory cloud. They come with Christ to enter a life that is part of a new order of things, a seventh dimension to creation.

plagioclase phenocryst in volcanic porphyry

summit banquet

your blessing is a manna madness that frees you to be fiercely honest
with your destiny and to force people to face the truth you are

basalt

manna madness

Make me like Moses, Lord.
Give me the courage
to tell you what I think
and then tell you off.

Give me Moses' madness,
his manna madness,
his wild scream of inner pain
that shows you
what it's like to be human
when we do what you ask.

Send me a spirit
to expose the sickness
of those who live by miracles
but eat them with as much respect
as stale hot dogs.

I want to scream at your people.
They have tasted the miracle
of your resurrection.
They know we are part
of a new dimension to life,
the seventh dimension,
the kingdom of Christ that surges
in, with, and under all things.

They have been given eternity
but they keep it for their retirement
sometime after death.

Make me like John the Baptist
with his wild honey madness,
his drive to announce the fire
that must purge God's people
before the new world
breaks completely through the surface.

I want no banquet of quail, Lord.
I want a holy madness
that can live on manna
in our wilderness
of concrete blocks and steel.

numbers 11:4-15

22

*Life in the new order means daring
integrity before God. Dining on his
manna produces a Moses madness, a
fierce impulse to be honest with God.
And the madness makes us human.*

june 4-10   your blessing is a snake dance performed to quell fears and phobias
deep in your being and bring the newborn you leaping into life

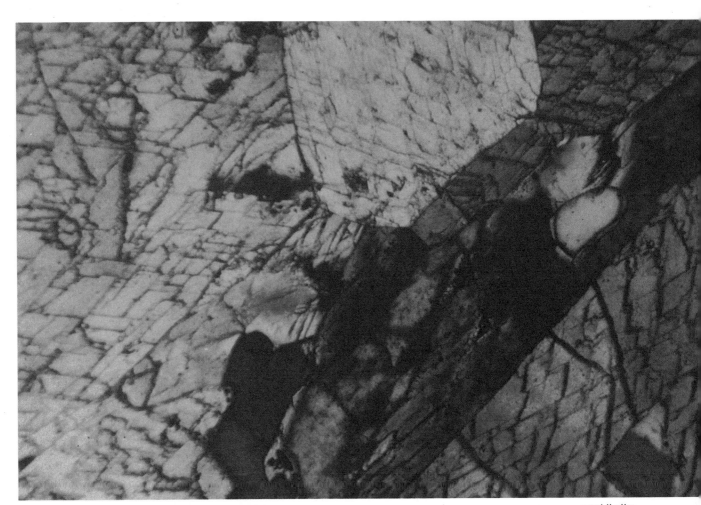

amphibolite

Snake dance

Lord, I'm scared.
I'm afraid of evil snakes
and ugly sewer rats
that crawl out of the earth
from whence old Adam came.

They come with flickering poison
and eyes red with anger.

They stir shadows
that lurk in my mind:
the fear of disgrace,
the fear of cold death,
and the fear of old sins
rising to poison my life.

My fears are vicious, Lord,
and wounds heal slowly.

Lift the snake for me.
Lift it high
so that I can behold the evil I fear
and look it in the eye.

Lift my eyes
that I might have the faith
to see my fears unfounded
and my sins helpless in the dust.

Let me feel you raising me
deep within
and lifting the evil high
for all to laugh at.

Lift me,
a cripple, from my chair
and teach me to dance,
aware of the fireworks on high
and unafraid of the snakeskins
shed at my feet.

numbers 21:4-9

23

The new life is a dangerous snake dance, a victory celebration over fear and death while Moses holds the bronze serpent aloft for faith to see.

your blessing is a fire voice that burns furiously in your soul
to change your old self through a penetrating forgiveness

Lord,
it's so much easier to say,
God is love
than God is fire.
It's so much nicer to hear
your voice in soft tones
than in fierce thunder claps
from a mountain fire.

What about the fire?
Have I run from the real God
whose silent fire burns
in, with, and under the universe?
Have I closed my ears
to the fire voice
that groans to be heard
through every sound of nature?

deuteronomy 4:32-40

Have I missed the meaning
of Christ's kingdom on earth
because love has become
but a drug the lonely seek?
Have I closed my eyes
to the fire that makes
genuine life possible?

Make your love deeper than words
like, "Pardon me!"
or "So sorry, Jesus."
Make forgiving a fire
in my voice
that changes me when I speak it
and changes my friends
when I really do it.

Make forgiveness a birth
into the kingdom of new life.
Make it a painful giving
of a personal part of me
that really belongs to another.

24

*Those in the new order of creation
grow by the fire of his forgiveness that
pierces deep as it changes us into
mountain climbers... high above
Sinai where unicorns canter.*

Forgive me, Lord,
with the fire of morning thunder.

Fire Voice

mica schist

your blessing is an eagle wind that lifts you violently to a
new dimension of flight with a rending resurrection blast

june 18-24

deuteronomy 32:7-14

25

Eagle winds rather than angel wings express the surging joy of our resurrection to life. Like Israel we are found by an eagle God and rescued from the desert by a violent wind.

I love to watch eagles, Lord,
as they spiral high
in the wind currents of heaven,
the life streams
that merge with mystery.

The eagles see the story below
better than we do.
Their vision penetrates the air
and catches a fresh reflection
of another dimension to life.

Like an eagle you found Israel,
born of a rock,
an orphan people in the howling sands.
Like an eagle they experienced you
swirling in from the sky
to love them
and lift them
higher and higher
to ride on sacred summits.

Come alive as an eagle in me
that I may experience you
as more than a desert dream.
Send an eagle wind,
the spirit of the risen Christ
sweeping in from his empty rock
to lift me higher and higher.

Let me feel anew laden souls
rising from the sand
to live with you.

Encircle me
and help me relive my new birth.
No, rather,
let me be born again of rock,
found again
and daily soar on eagle wings
to dwell where eagles watch,
talking with the sky
about your new world
hidden below.

eagle winds

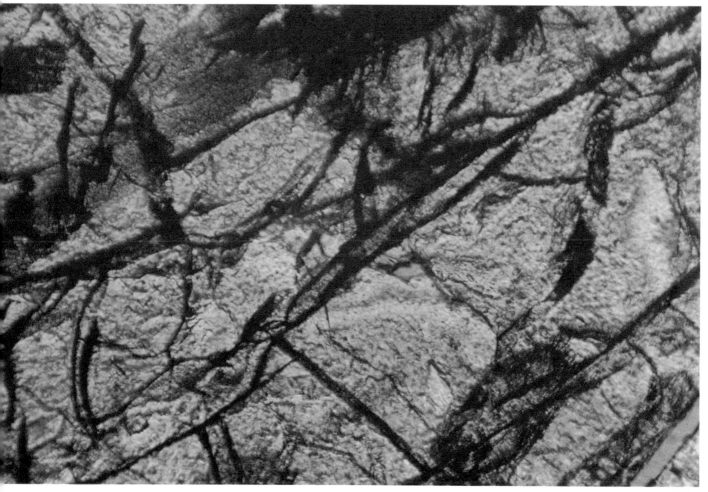

olivine

your blessing is a Canaan dew charged with ancient mystery and
ready for the pangs of your baptism to new life and dancing at dawn

june 25-july 1

deuteronomy 33:26-29

*We are baptized into a new life with a
holy dew, a Canaan dew charged with
mystery and birthquake power.*

Those Israelites, Lord,
they knew how to praise.
They knew how to make a homecoming
a hymn to remember.

When they hit the land
.they hailed you as the hero,
the wild rider of the skies
racing your chariot cloud
aloud
and splashing fireworks
across the laughing sky.

They said you threw a banquet
called Canaan,
a land lush with life,
bubbling with milk
and aged with golden wines.

You baptized it with dew,
a magic moisture
charged with blessing
and the power to raise the lifeless.

Drop your dew among us now
and give life to the shadows of hope
that linger within us
like the memory of childhood games.

Call us back to Canaan
and let the dew of heaven
baptize our spirits
to rouse the mystery of life in us.
Call us back to say thanks
for Canaan and cactus plants,
for cuts and purple bruises,
and for homecoming songs of hope.

Let us hold a new banquet
for the homecoming of **Christ**;
let us dance in the graveyards
where the new dew is falling
and the new world is breaking through
beginning with me
and you.

serpentized olivine

Canaan dew

mica schist

your blessing is hosanna canyon where you shout forth your tomorrow
and the resounding echoes shatter the past that would silence your birth

joshua 3:7-17

hosanna canyon

27

Life in Christ means welcoming Christ and walking the long road of history with him. It means walking hosanna free through the Jordan River, the Holy City, and tomorrow's deep canyons.

What an advent, Lord.
Joshua led the way
through the great Jordan canyon
with the holy ark ahead
and the desert far behind.

"Hosanna," they cried,
"The Lord of earth has come.
The living God is here."

What an advent, Lord.
Jesus led the way
through the mighty gates of Zion
with his horrible death ahead
and his safety far behind.

"Hosanna," they cried,
and the cries still echo
through the canyons of time:
"Hosanna!
Hosanna!
The liberator comes!"

Enter the canyons we travel
and let your promise echo
like thunder
to shatter the shackles,
the chains from our past
that try to rule our lives.

Lead the way to the future
far from the people
and the past
that try to claim us.

Let us hear hosannas fall
green and gold
across our canyon
and echo with the dawn:
Hosanna!
Hosanna!
I'm free!
I'm born!

joshua 10:6-14

your blessing is a sun day, a threatening day when the sun stands still
and you have the chance to face eternity free from the terror of death

With the sun and the moon, Lord,
you fought for your people
to win them the land of Canaan.

Will the sun stand still again
on the day you return?
Will you storm in from space
clothed in solar fire?

Sad to say, Lord,
your second coming does not move us.
We don't live by the sun,
watching for spots
that signal your arrival.

Should we?

july 9-15

Or is the problem in the way
we understand your first coming?
Do we fail to see the shrill signs
that sweep the sky
because we do not grasp the deeper hope
that came alive when you first came?

Lord, make today Sun Day,
the dawn of a new beginning,
a bright new birth.
Give us the inner awareness
that our new life in you
is the start of an even greater creation.

28

*Walking with Christ in the new order
of creation enables us to see creation
with new eyes. The exploding sun and
the wind flame sky accompany us to
point the way of his coming.*

Come, Sun of Righteousness,
and rise on high
from within every particle
hidden in the universe
and blaze for us
a new day.

basalt porphyry

sun day

july 16-22   your blessing is a life light that tears away your gaudy masks
and shines intensely on your inner face, exposed but free

In the twentieth century, Lord,
angels are embarrassing.
They emerge from light
and vanish in flames
. . . but not on our street.

They are secret life forces,
lights vibrating
in every crevice of creation.

Yet angels don't trouble us quite as much
as men like Samson or John the Baptist
whose birth the angels announce.

judges 13:2-20

Those people are so intense,
so different,
so deeply aware of your will,
so driven by your pulse,
so full of your piercing light
that we shrink from them
. . . when they walk down our street.

Are you, Lord Jesus,
are you as intense as they?
And would you have us that way?

Come and show us.
You are the light of life,
the light behind light itself.

Send your light to expose us,
to uncover our inner selves
lying huddled beneath the dark masks
we have molded to hide ourselves.

29   *Walking the way of Christ's coming
means meeting the men of his coming,
men like Samson and John. They
possess a harsh life light from him that
cuts through our pretenses and calls us
to be true.*

Come with your light
and make us alive to our inner selves,
alive to your word of new life,
alive and intense
as your light penetrates through us
to expose others masked with smiles.

Life Light

pyroxene gabbro

july 23-29   your blessing is the flame flesh you share with Adam and the
Indians, with oppressed and poor, with the gentle and God himself

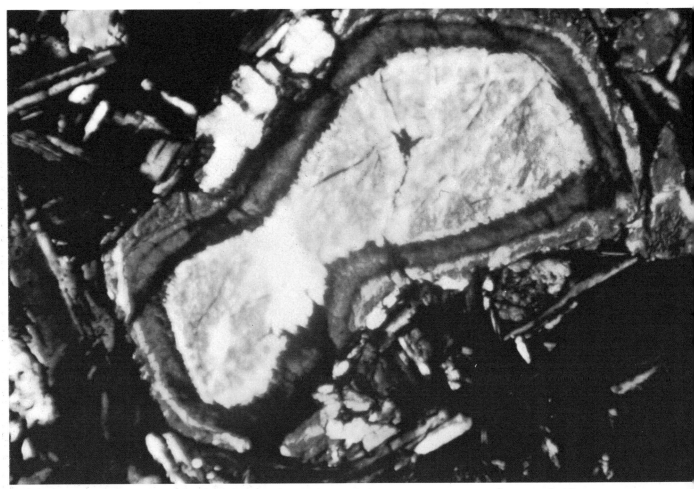

reaction rim on pyroxene

Flame Flesh

It makes me furious, Lord,
when people treat me
as if I am nothing.

I burn with shame
when my Indian companions,
my black brothers and sisters,
or my foreign friends
are treated like dirt.

They have the wrong family tree,
they belong to the wrong race.
And so do you, Lord Jesus.
You're nobody.

Your line has black sheep like Adam,
white murderers like David,
liars like Jacob,
and dark strangers like Ruth.
Why, Boaz bought that foreign girl
along with a plot of land
after a wild night on the threshing floor!

ruth 4:1-11

You certainly didn't pick your ancestors!
Or did you?

You came as nobody
to give anyone without hope
the joy of discovering
that it's a gift to be born,
a privilege to be human,
and an honor to be the person you are.

But more than that!
You became flesh of my flesh,
my family tree of sinners,
fools, and oppressed.
You came to give them dignity,
to set them free from fear,
and instil in them the power
to live a new life
where love means liberation.

30

The flame becomes flesh and dwells among us. Our Man comes!

In you I have worth.
I am somebody!

july 30-august 5

your blessing is a somersault rock that tips your old world upside down and forces you to find yourself in a new role called openness

pyroxene gabbro

somersault rock

1 samuel 2:1-10

There is no rock like you, Lord,
and yet every rock on earth
is alive
with the mystery of your touch.

You do not come to be a warm refuge,
a velvet rock that makes us secure
or keeps things just as they are.
You somersault into our lives
like a superball.
You come to change roles,
to turn this world upside down,
to upset the apple cart.

You come to crack down
on the greedy and the arrogant,
to break the will
of those who love war,
to force the wealthy to scrounge,
to give the barren children,
to find love for the lonely,
to lift the abused from the ashes,
and raise the oppressed from hell
to give them seats of power.

You come to reverse the roles
of God and man,
to upset the order of creation.
You, our Creator,
became a creature called Jesus Christ.

You moved from God to man,
from ancient rock to soft flesh.
You came an eternal seed,
to penetrate all flesh,
all rock,
and bring new creations into being.

Reverse the roles among us now.
Upset our lives with the new
and dwell in flesh among us,
to begin tomorrow your way.
Your way, Lord!
Your way!

31

This man called Christ is a somersault rock who invades the old creation, upsetting the old order of things. The new order is here, the kingdom has come and roles are being reversed.

your blessing is a falling star that descends from spurious splendor to enter your crib of conflict and rise to your birth

august 6-12

1 samuel 4:15-20

calcite

When roles are reversed, stars collide and fall. All creation becomes a sign for those in Christ.

Stars are for wishing,
say the superstitious,
and falling stars for dreams.

What do you say, Lord?

I wish for so many things,
for a life free from hatred
and a land free from war.

I set you high in my sky,
a gleaming North Star
with all heaven revolving
in harmony around you.

Then suddenly you fall,
you lose,
you let my world crumble.

Like the day you let the Philistines
capture your sacred throne,
the symbol of your epiphany to Israel.
And people began to call their children
names like, "No More Glory,"
"God is Dead,"
and "Hiroshima."

You don't do things my way, Lord!
You are so free,
free to fall and fail,
free to be disgraced and disappear.
Then suddenly you reappear
where no one expects you.

Like when you rise in the East,
bouncing around as a stainless star
that falls in Bethlehem
with superstitious wise men
trailing in its train.

It's ridiculous!
It's the way you do things.
It's the clue to your new world.

Star

Lord, I want to change.
I want to be transformed
like light through rock crystal.
I want to be made a new person
with real integrity.

I want to be able to taste the mystery,
to know the meaning of new life,
to experience through and through
that I am in Christ,
in the seventh dimension of life,
in his kingdom.

But I cannot feel it.
Why, Lord, why?

Old Samuel anointed your David
with holy oil
and David was a different man.
The Spirit coursed through him
like lightning at midnight.

1 samuel 16:10-13

He knew that God had made him over,
that a creation was happening
inside of him.
He could feel the birthquakes
of his new life.

Do the same for me.
It's midnight!
Anoint me into a free me,
a new me.

I want to be so changed
that I won't just do what others say
or be what the world wants me to be,
but be my true self in Christ.

Whether I feel it or not,
make it happen, Lord.

Or has it been happening
and I have refused to let the new life surface
or let the Spirit complete
what has already begun in me?

33

The struggle to know our true selves intensifies as we move from birth to birth in Christ. The same holy wind that once stirred David moves us to rise at midnight and anoint our souls with hope.

august 13-19   your blessing is a midnight oil prepared to anoint you with a new spirit
that will course headlong through your tortured being like lightning

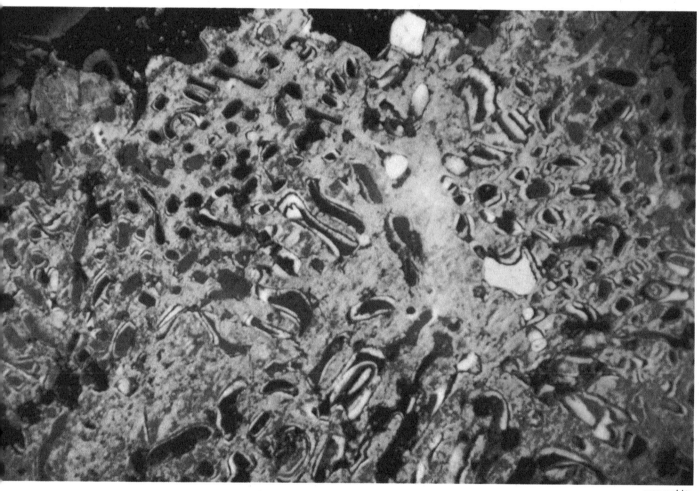

myrmekite

obsidian

august 20-26   your blessing is a celebration way, a journey from the turmoil of self-discovery to the explosive celebration of self-assurance

Celebration Way

Today we celebrate, Lord!
We acclaim your glory
as we remember our agony.

Writhe with us, Lord,
as we strain to be born,
as we feel the pain of self-discovery,
as we taste the bile of self-rejection,
as we hear the voice of self-accusation,
and long for release.

Dance with us, Lord,
as we break forth from the womb,
as we affirm who we are
as we find our freedom in you.

Dance with us, Lord,
as we dance King David's dance
on the high holy ground
before the gleaming ark of your presence.

Dance with us, Lord,
as the stars above dance in chorus,
the seas swirl with rhythm,
the winds sing through the woods,
the lizards laugh by the roadside,
and wine winks with excitement.

Be our peace offering, Lord,
and commune with us at your table
where your body and blood are free.
Give us the peace of a new life,
the forgiven life in Christ,
the life where love means
joy at the deeps of despair.

Walk the new way of life with us
and make it a celebration way
from the caverns of despair
to the ridges of self-assurance in you.

2 samuel 6:12-19

34

The turmoil of growth in self-discovery and self-awareness leads to a new self-assurance in Christ. He dances with us down celebration way through the pain of new birth.

Lord, how do we live by promise
when all around promises are broken
and trust means the same as "sucker!"

Bulbs live by the promise of spring,
and birds by a winter promise
of sunshine somewhere down South.
Flowers live by the promise of rain
and roots by an underground promise
of warm moisture from the rocks.

But what is a promise for me, Lord?
A welcome word from a friend?.
An inner outreach from someone I trust?
A word from the soul of another,
a word today I can act on tomorrow?

Your promise is that and more,
for your word asks me to believe you
when everyone else seems to live
by the laws of hard-core reality.

I strain to believe you, Lord,
like a bird caught in a hurricane.

You promised David a son
and sons for his son
who would be your sons
and channels of blessing for Israel.
People lived by that promise
until the day of the great surprise
when a son of God arrived
who was *the* Son of God,
Jesus Christ, the Promise!

august 27-september 2

your blessing is an underground promise that reaches for
an orange sun from deep in the hard rock of cold reality

2 samuel 7:1-16

Underground promise

May that promise surge faith in me
to believe I too am a child in Christ.

Confirm in me your promise
that at the core of hard-core reality
there lives a word of promise
that enables all reality to be
and new reality to rise even in me.

35

Celebrating life in the seventh dimension means living by an underground promise. Like David we trust the promise and wait for the sun. At the hard core of reality Christ is creating a new world.

staurolite gneiss

your blessing is a storm comet plunging through the chaos waters
to snatch you from dragon jaws and sweep you to freedom

My lord,
angels of evil are working on me,
leering at my freedom,
convulsing the waters of chaos
and the tentacles of death
with spasms of evil desire.

Angels of death come in white,
in uniforms of government
and clergy robes,
in the promises of politicians
and the deceit of greedy men.

Evil strains
to destroy the new life within me.

How will you rescue me?

2 samuel 22:1-20

With the quiet comfort of a friend
in the still of night?
With the gentleness of companions
ready to cry while I die?

I tire of quiet waiting for peace,
and silent suffering amid turmoil.
I long for the King of the storm
to shake his fist with justice.

Leave your invisible abode, Lord,
and storm in under orange skies.
Send cherub flames and seraph winds
and ride your angry black clouds.
Hit the heavens with your storm comet
and spit white lightning where it hurts.

Split the ocean bed apart
and reach to the grey deeps
to free me.
Turn chaos into a toy
and send it home with its dragontail
between its lumpy legs.
Lock evil in its cave
and set my boat free to sail
where whitecaps sing halleluja.

*When chaos storms threaten our new
life and the menacing deep rises in
soul or society, the Lord of the storm
rides as he did of old. He reveals
himself in the very struggle for freedom.*

Storm Comet

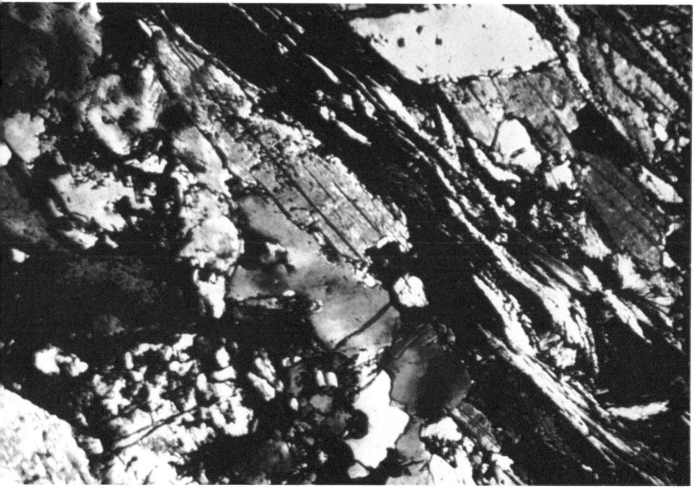

mica schist

september 10-16 your blessing is a vineyard altar where you are summoned to crush
grapes with Elijah and drink wine aged for life beyond your crushing

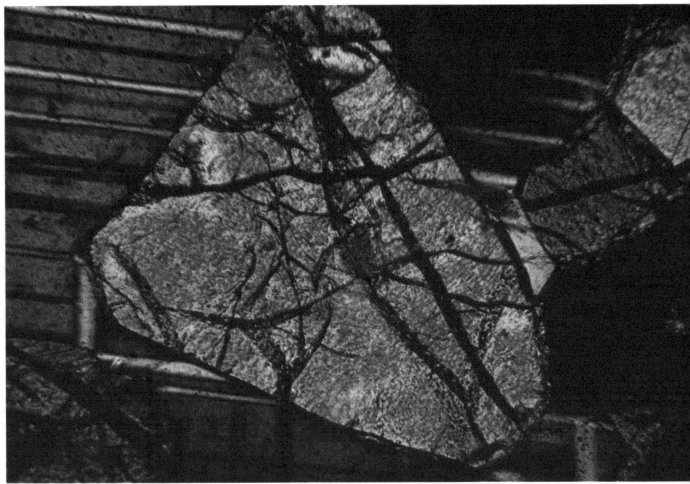

olivine gabbro

1 kings 18:36-46

37

*Our struggle for full freedom in the
new creation means a call for prophets
to come to the vineyard altar and
crush grapes with Elijah. The blood
stains on the altar cry out for strong
justice and human equity.*

Vineyard Altar

A voice from the vineyard calls,
calls in the crisp of evening,
calls me to be a prophet
and speak a word that draws blood
. . . my blood.

The prophets around me lie dumb.
Will you protest their stoning,
their abuse by landlords,
church lords,
and society lords?

Your call is a call to be true,
true to your truth,
to come to the vineyard altar
where prophets gave their lives
and old Elijah waits
to crush grapes at dawn.

Will I be crushed by stones
on that altar?

Before me I see a sacrifice,
Jesus, your Son,
the heir of the vineyard,
the Man of Truth.

He offers me wine with his blood,
his blood with wine . . . and I flinch.
He offers me life,
life aged with wine,
life beyond this crushing.

A cloud on the red horizon hovers
ready to baptize the morning
with raindrops and new vines,
with blessings in good wine . . .
before the altar,
the rock who is Christ himself.

Free me to be true, Lord,
to be a prophet
before the vineyard altar of Christ,
where life is drunk
more deeply than death.

your blessing is a still small echo deep within that heightens the senses
of your soul to the inner music of life rising in the new creation

There are times, Lord,
when I pause in the quiet fog
with lights crisp as crystal,
or watch a mountain lake at dawn;
I wonder at the silent music,
the calm that murmurs
"magic."

It's as though I am aware
for the first time in my life
that I am alive.
My breathing is the only sound
in the stillness.
Even my thoughts vibrate too loudly
for the soft air.

I am caught unawares
at the dawn of creation
where all was yet motionless
and no bird,
no human footstep had fallen.

Your word is then in me
like a swelling seed
after the spring storms.

I know for an instant
that Christ is an echo within
saying,
"Adam, my son!
You are as new in me
as you are in the magic of creation,
you are as alive with my new life
as you are with the life of the first creation.

Come leave your quivering cave.
There are others who need
to hear that word
and feel the seed of new life in me,
the magic of Life amid life."

Lord, lead me from life to Life,
from magic to maturity.

still small echo

1 kings 19:9-18

38

At the eye of the human hurricane a still small echo calls us from our caves to summon God's people to courage in Christ, courage to affirm the worth of all life.

plagioclase and quartz

september 24-30   your blessing is a seventh dimension to life, a new creation for
                   you to experience by fire in, with, and under the present world

micropegmatite

seuenth dimension

There are times, Lord,
when I am completely out of it.
It's as though I am struck blind
and insensitive
to anything but the cold world,
the lifeless life I enjoy.

I no longer see through a glass darkly,
catching a glimpse of your coming.
My glass is opaque
and my faith seems fake.

Open my eyes, Lord,
to the inner mystery of creation,
to the mountains on fire with angels,
to skies in flux with the spirit,
to rocks in ferment with hope.

Open my eyes
to the seventh dimension,
to that new world of Christ operating
in, with, and under this world,
to that resurrection power
transforming things from death to life,
to that new order of existence
in which old lives are liberated,
to that new reality in Christ
erupting at the core of all reality.

Open my eyes
to the Christ who is changing everything
in his church and his world,
in me and my world.

Open my eyes with love,
not the love of polite pastors
or even kind souls,
but the love that burns away my blindness
and opens my soul.
Heal me with the love of Christ
who became blind through death
that my eyes might be open to life
in him.

2 kings 6:15-23

39

Life in the new creation is life in the seventh dimension. Christ is creating a new world in our old. He is changing everything. With eyes wide open we behold mountains on fire with angel glory.

your blessing is a wilderness courtship where you discover anew what it
means to have radical respect for yourself in a life of trusting others

october 1-7

hosea 2:9-20

4O

*When we are tempted to desert the
community of the new creation for
the good old days of life by greed, we
are summoned to the wilderness
where the courtship is tough but true.*

Lord,
take me back to the wilderness
where the test is true.

Strip me, if need be,
of the sweet things I cherish,
the parties, the presents,
and the greed society
I secretly love and live by.

Take me to the wilderness
where the showdown happens,
where nothing survives but the sun
and the stones
and the demons of the desert.

Take me back with Israel
whom you stripped of all her glory,
her high standard of living,
and left in a desert to repent.

Take me back to the wilderness
to hear again your words of courtship,
your vow of new life for Israel.
Let me hear your promise of a new world,
a new covenant with all of nature
where the greed society will die
and life on earth would be peace.

Work in me a deep repentance
that means giving up
more than tips and toys.
Effect an inner surrender,
an inner change of direction.

Teach me to live with a radical respect
of myself and others,
and not be pressured by approval
to be someone I am not.

Let me see that new life now
alive in those who repent,
alive through Christ, the victor
over the ultimate temptation
to live by greed instead of grace.

Wilderness Courtship

olivine gabbro

We live, Lord,
in a land of angry people.

Some explode with anger
pent up through years of humiliation.
Others respond with anger
born of unseen guilt.
Some draw anger like fire
and others suppress it like death.
Some live by anger
and some die from it.
Life itself seems angry!

How do we handle their anger, Lord,
. . . and yours?

In your anger you destroyed a people,
the ten tribes of Israel,
and left but a few lost sheep.
In your anger you sent lions
to frighten the lawless.
When you are angry
our anger smacks of rebellion.

Do we need to become little dogs
eating the crumbs of your banquet table
before we can find hope?
Are you the sole avenger
when injustice and evil
burn out of control among us?

Or can we live with Christ
as an angry Jesus
who rapped the disciples' knuckles,
cracked leaders' heads together,
and exposed the masks of the nice people?

In the new life we live in you
give us the mind to discern
between the angers that invade
and the angers that erupt within us.
And help us to learn what it means
to be angry lions for you
rather than lap dogs of society
fed on weak love.

2 kings 17:19-28

*Life in Christ does not mean a re-
sponse of weak love but a lion anger
of strong love defending the defense-
less and condemning every act of
dehumanization. With the Lord of
Israel we demand radical respect for
human life and human worth.*

41

october 8-14   your blessing is a lion anger erupting from deep within the new you
against every injustice and dehumanization of those striving to be true

biotite gneiss

Lion anger

october 15-21   your blessing is a piercing earth wail calling you to be the finger of God that casts out the demons of corruption rampant in the earth

hornblende and myrmekite

I listen to the earth, Lord,
and I hear a piercing wail,
a universe convulsing with sorrow.

I see the vision of Jeremiah
where darkness hangs like death
and the earth dies desolate,
not from some swift atomic shock
but a slow corruption.
I see a world waste with waste
and void of love for all that lives,
a world without wild flowers
or people fingering the warm soil.

If all the birds stopped singing,
would anyone notice?
Is there one person in town
who would exchange his car for a tree?
Is there one man who loves justice enough
to cast out the very demons
he harbors in his house?

Our society is a sham, Lord,
a company of respectable hypocrites
who refuse to risk their good names
for the wailing earth.

Will you come again
to cast out demons in our society?
Do we possess the resurrection power
to remove the cancer of pollution
and the demons of injustice?
Is the new life we have in you
more than a vague inner dream?

If it is, Lord,
then make us exorcists!
Make us the finger of God
to cast out every demon of evil,
pollution, and injustice we harbor.
Make us signs of the kingdom of God,
the new universe being born
from this corroding creation.

jeremiah 4:23-5:5

The new creation groans beneath the wailing of our earth where demons of death and corruption are now fed by greedy men. In Christ we are the finger of God to cast out such demons.

your blessing is a firstborn freedom in which you are born anew with
the right to be free and the courage to risk your life for the broken

jeremiah 31:1-9

What does it mean to be free, Lord,
in the land of the brave and the free
where the free are slaves of fear and folly?

Where is the deeper freedom
that comes from the courage to be
the very persons we are
and risk everything on that?

Why do so many still like
to make others feel small or inferior?
Why do so many who love Christ
still love to put people in their place
and keep them there?

Where is that love of liberation
that comes through Christ within us?

Take me back to walk with Israel
who lived by the promise of firstborn freedom
and life after death in exile.

Take me back to plant vines and dance
with Samaritans on their mountain,
or eat the sacrament with thousands
on the hillsides of Galilee.

Let me walk with the lame and the blind,
with the vast company of the unclean
who return free from exile
and know the Lord as their liberator.

Make my freedom firstborn
with all the rights to live free,
with a deep conviction of who I am
and how to live by freedom.

You, Lord Jesus Christ,
you were the one man truly free.
Make me free in you
and give me the power to free others
with the message of your love.

43

We also groan beneath the hand of those who use their freedom to imprison the hearts and lives of others. True freedom is freedom in Christ. From his hand we celebrate the sacrament as a festival of freedom.

basalt

Firstborn Freedom

october 29-november 4   your blessing is a new human planted within you that knows an inner
worth, lives by an inner truth, and beats with empathy for all flesh

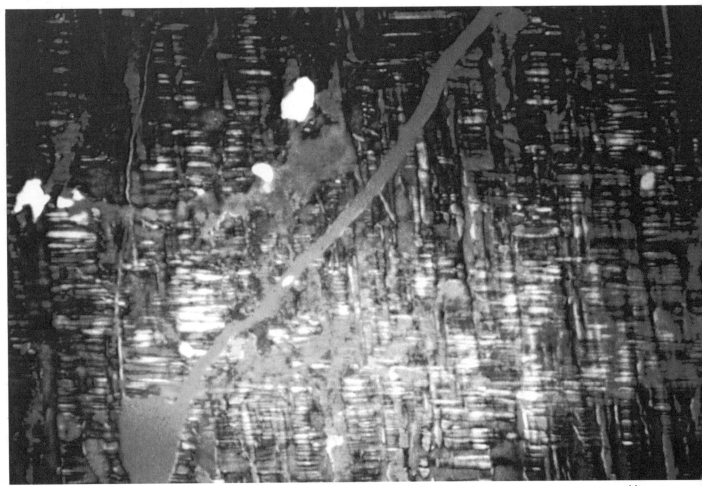

perthite

new human

In the promises of Jeremiah, Lord,
you promised to change the inner me
and free me from the words of the law
that stand out there
demanding
and demanding
a test I always fail.

You promised, Lord,
to implant in me a new human
who is part of your new humanity
where your word is a drive in the heart
and not a threat on the books.
You promised
that I would experience you in person.

jeremiah 31:31-34

You promised, Lord,
the kind of penetrating forgiveness
that makes us free men and women
belonging to the new order of existence,
the new order of life
where we know our true selves
by knowing your love deep within us.

You promised, Lord!
Keep your promises with us now.

Lord Jesus Christ,
you came as the one true fulfillment
of those fabulous promises.
You came the one truly free human
who knew God without appeal to others.
You were the first true member
of the new humanity.

Mediate for us now, Lord Jesus,
and make the new humanity happen here.
It began with you.
Make it alive again in us.

44

The new order of things is a new humanity. Through the blood of the new covenant, new humans live forgiven in Christ. They strain to be human in an inhuman society.

Let me be born a new human
through the blood of the new covenant,
the True Man of the new humanity,
and the forgiveness he offers.

november 5-11 your blessing is the bittersweet applause you hear as you rise above encouragement from others to integrity within yourself

isaiah 49:1-13

As servants of Christ applause is bittersweet like the accolades our Lord received on Palm Sunday. Life in the new order of things is fed by integrity from Christ, not by approval from peers or applause from friends.

We love our heroes, Lord,
the champions of the earth.
We long for the roar of the crowd
with our own name on its lips . . .
even if the crowd is only one.

Your way is different, Lord.
You meet us as a miserable servant,
a hero who is no hero.
You come empty of glory,
empty!

You come to fail!

"Hero," cry the people,
"Marvelous Messiah.
Magnificent Champion."

Amid the bittersweet applause
you hear another chorus rise,
"Fallen Idol!
Traitor!
Crucify Him!"

In the air there hangs the expectation
of a bitter hour with death
and a later hour without the crowd,
an hour of quiet surprise
when a few who follow discover
that with God
the sweet is drawn from the bitter,
salvation is found in his suffering Son,
life is born in death.

There was no reporter at the resurrection,
no applause from the crowd,
only the almost uncontrollable clapping
of earth and sky
in the bittersweet dawn.

Walk your way with me, Lord,
without the applause of the crowd.
Teach me to live a servant role,
ready to face death
to express your love alive in me.

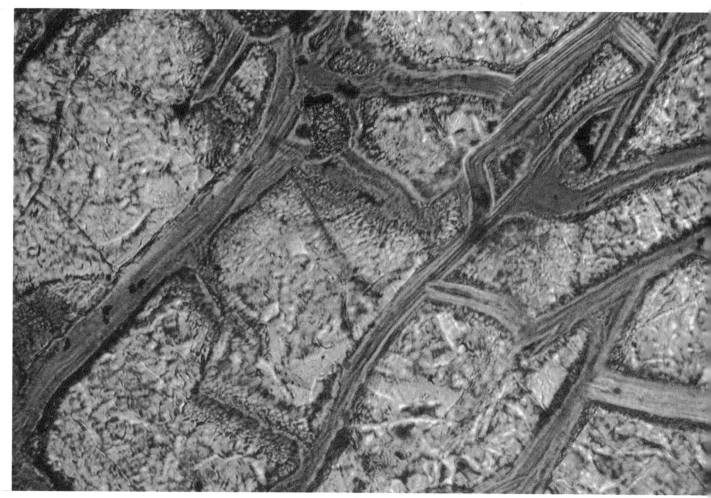

serpentized olivine

bittersweet applause

november 12-18   your blessing is a resurrection rampage at large in the world summoning you to leave all and shout YES at the birth of the new creation

resurrection rampage

ezekiel 37:1-10

46   *Life in the seventh dimension is life by resurrection. A resurrection rampage is loose in the valley of bones causing birthquakes and births everywhere. The butterfly sky is high, the flood birds are soaring, and new humans are shouting: "The word is YES! The Son is up!"*

I hear old knuckles knocking
as soft breathing stirs the bones
in resurrection valley.

I watch a wisp of dawn wind
squirrel its way across my yard
and gently whisper,
Yes!
The word is YES.
The Son is up!

The word is YES!
Life is up!

YES, cry the skies.
YES, roar the deeps.
YES, ring the rafters.
YES, sing the snows.

YES, quake the canyons.
YES, cheer the beaks
of a thousand baby birds
and a hundred mountain peaks.

"YES," says God.
"My Son is up.
He's out of death.

The word is UP!
My Son is YES!

"His resurrection is on a rampage,
an outbreak of new births
dancing through the earth."

Let that YES be ours every day.
The word is YES.
We are up,
up with the Son,
up despite every down.

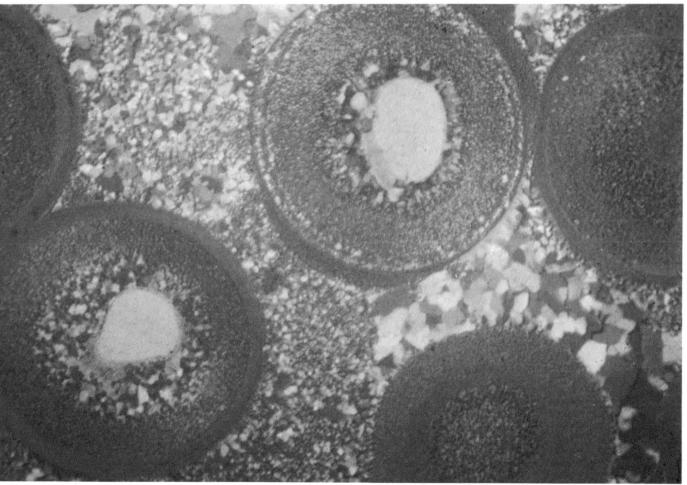

oolite

hornblende andesite

Peace Scar

your blessing is a peace scar you will feel seared in your heart when you rise from rending doubt to risking faith

ezekiel 36:22-32

47 Those who lie exhausted from the resurrection rampage are met by a man with peace scars. The new life he offers means peace with scars, resurrection through repeated dying.

Man of Scars,
we shrink from a scar-torn face
or beauty rent by red tissue.
Disfigured faces are a barrier to love,
a brutal lash of fate
we secretly fear.

Man of Scars,
let us know you without the glow
of an unreal resurrection.
Meet us with your torn body,
your gashed hands,
your broken flesh.

Man of Scars,
come to us in the night
when your death is but a distant dream
and your resurrection a lingering doubt.
Come and touch us
with your scars.

Man of Scars,
when our guilt and fears terrify us,
show us the scars of our sin
borne in your body for us.
Show us the red welts of death
from which life flowed for us.

Man of Scars,
give us the courage
to behold ourselves in the glass
and see the face of our false beauty.

Help us affirm the scars of death
we feel
as a new heart is planted within us
and we are born again in you.

Risen Man of Scars,
let us see the beauty of your wounds,
the meaning of life for death,
the peace scars of victory.
Through them let us rise
to overcome the world
and crush our doubts.

november 26-december 2   your blessing is a space festival to which you are invited to celebrate living by breaking out with thunder from your old selfish self

micropegmatite

space festival

zechariah 9:16-10:1

Good Shepherd,
amid the battering winds of crime
and the ugly smell of evil,
it's time for a festival.

Open space, Lord,
sing the future with us
and celebrate the birth of life.

Call the birds to bless us,
the orchards to blossom,
the springs to sparkle,
and galaxies to burst with glory.

Take us to new fields
far from our warm confining fold.

Let us hear the overture of new space
as an invitation to peace,
an invitation to the resurrection festival
of Christ the Shepherd.

Adorn the shepherd tree
where you died
to bring us life and space.

Celebrate the festival with us
and fill us with a deep sense of humor
to laugh at death
and dance in the midst of disaster.

Let us behold again
our new life in Christ
as part of the new order everywhere,
the new creation among men.
Let us see how space itself
unites with us
and life rises with us
in a worldwide festival
of praise to the Shepherd of Life.

Let our space festival be a sign
that birth is redeemed from death
to celebrate with us
our resurrection in the Lord.

48

Resurrection is a space festival for the community of Christ in the new creation. Our risen Lord is the Good Shepherd who invites us to laugh amid despair and dance on the mound where death is buried.

december 3-9   your blessing is a black spring that fountains forth from the dark deeps of birth in death to refresh you with living joy

zechariah 14:1-9

49   *At the festival we drink from a black spring that surges forth from the black depths of birth at the center of the new creation.*

Take us to the spring, Lord,
the black spring of living water,
the fountain of life from the deep,
where we celebrate your resurrection.

Take us to the holy hill
where the spring sparkles free.
Let us drink deeply of a joy
that overflows within
like the spirit of a child at a fair.

We are surrounded by your gifts,
your goodness and grace,
and yet our spirit fades.

The routine rules our minds
and the tedious governs our time.
The jostle of climbers
and the lust of losers
trouble our slipping souls.
We lose sight of you for a while
and then a while longer.
We fume with frustration
as we rush madly
from nowhere to nowhere.

At the end we simply sigh!
We are lost in a maze
of swiveling ways.

Come and refresh us
with the joy of your resurrection,
with the taste of new songs
that erupt in the hour of travail.
Guide us to life
when death envelops our minds.

Help us see the new creation happening
in our struggle to be.

King of the Hill,
may our new birth be true
at the festival spring of life
with you.

obsidian

black spring

your blessing is a wind truth that cuts through your crust of lies to bring alive an inner truth that makes you true in the new creation

Lord of the winds,
you promised to come
as the wind truth of life.

You promised to come
from the first breath at creation
down through the lazy lines of history
and then through Jesus Christ.

Blow now, Wind Truth.
Stir my whole being
to be true
and speak the truth
that others may be true
to themselves
and you.

joel 2:28-33

As this endless cycle of lies
revolves around me
and distorts the truth,
come, Wind Truth,
and clear the poisonous air.

Come
and confront me with Jesus Christ,
the enemy of the lie,
the way to the truth
of new birth through death,
his death.

Give me the faith
to survive the crucible of truth
as your wind
cuts deeply through the crust
of lies that surrounds me.

A wind truth from Christ cuts sharply into those who drink at the black spring. In the wind truth there is danger and a dream, courage and kindness, rage and respect.

Breathe in me new life,
true life,
born of fire and the Spirit,
the Wind Truth
sent from Jesus Christ.

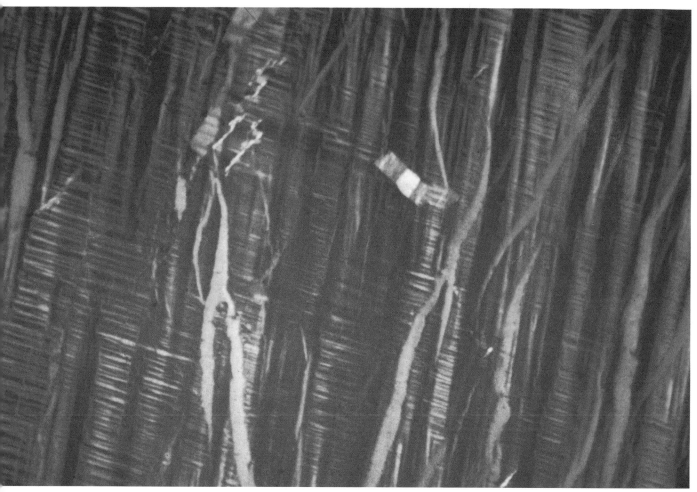

perthite

wind truth

december 17-23   your blessing is a volcano dawn erupting underground from
                  the womb of the morning to declare you ready for birth

psalm 110

You erupted, Lord,
as a human being,
as a child in a shed,
as a baby left crying
on the doorstep of earth.

You burst forth
from a deep dawn,
from the womb of the morning,
from the caverns of earth
where death swallows life.

You erupted
with wings of victory,
with birthquakes of triumph,
with stars as your crown,
with the mountains your footstool,
and life held high in your hand.

In the splendor of your struggle
let me find a place
where your risen power works
in my private conflict with death.

In the volcano dawn
of your eruption
let me see your light
in my tight corner.

Erupt in me.
Let the new life you bring
burst forth in me.
Erupt in me
with a volcano,
with a bold dawn,
with a deep explosion
that means a beginning,
a birth.

Ascend in me
that I might be born
and enjoy
a volcano dawn.

51

*A volcanic dawn explodes daily for
those who know life in the new creation. We rise free to be born.*

Volcano dawn

muscovite-garnet gneiss

andesite porphyry

december 24-31   your blessing is a Sky Father who makes your life a crucible
where new love is forged through his forgiving love for you

psalm 103

*Life in Christ is blessed by our Father,
whose love is deeper than the magic
deep and whose Son has overcome the
evil stampede for us. In Christ love
becomes a crucible for our birth as
new humans true to ourselves, our
Lord, and his new creation.*

Sky Father

Our Father,
Sky Father,
higher than high below
and deeper than deep above,
penetrate our lives with love.

You know we are dust
and dream of glistening glory,
you know we are clay,
children who keep changing their story.

Yet wherever we wonder,
from one brief year to the next,
leap the skies with your love,
and reshape our clumsy clay
in the image of your Son.

Come with your love,
stronger than hell
and deeper than death,
to alarm us with life
and shock us with freedom.

Implant in us the kind of love
that is forgiving not foolish,
confronting not cruel,
direct not devious.

Teach us to love
with honesty not flattery,
with empathy not kind lies,
with concern not sweet control.

Make our love a crucible,
a birth power from the Christ child,
a new creation as true human beings.

Make our birthquakes grow
with the birthquakes of the earth
until the universe exclaims,
"We're free!"
"We're born!"
"We're free!"

Church Year	Birthquake Theme
First in Advent	27. HOSANNA CANYON
Second in Advent	28. SUN DAY
Third in Advent	29. LIFE LIGHT
Fourth in Advent	1. WIND FLAME
Christmas Day	30. FLAME FLESH
First after Christmas	31. SOMERSAULT ROCK
The Name of Jesus	15. SILLY SEED
Second after Christmas	8. WHIRLWIND CLAY
Epiphany	32. FALLING STAR
First after Epiphany	33. MIDNIGHT OIL
Second after Epiphany	34. CELEBRATION WAY
Third after Epiphany	35. UNDERGROUND PROMISE
Fourth after Epiphany	36. STORM COMET
Fifth after Epiphany	37. VINEYARD ALTAR
Sixth after Epiphany	38. STILL SMALL ECHO
Seventh after Epiphany	39. SEVENTH DIMENSION
Eighth after Epiphany	20. MOLTEN THUNDER
Transfiguration	19. MOUNTAIN MAGIC
Ash Wednesday	22. MANNA MADNESS
First in Lent	40. WILDERNESS COURTSHIP
Second in Lent	41. LION ANGER
Third in Lent	42. EARTH WAIL
Fourth in Lent	43. FIRSTBORN FREEDOM
Fifth in Lent	44. NEW HUMAN
Palm Sunday	45. BITTERSWEET APPLAUSE
Maundy Thursday	21. SUMMIT BANQUET
Good Friday	9. SUFFERING TREE
Easter Day	46. RESURRECTION RAMPAGE
Second of Easter	47. PEACE SCAR
Third of Easter	48. SPACE FESTIVAL
Fourth of Easter	49. BLACK SPRING
Fifth of Easter	50. WIND TRUTH
Sixth of Easter	51. VOLCANO DAWN
Ascension	13. FLOOD BIRD
Seventh of Easter	52. SKY FATHER
Pentecost	1. WIND FLAME
First after Pentecost	2. MAGIC DEEP
Second after Pentecost	3. LIGHTNING WORD
Third after Pentecost	4. BUTTERFLY SKY
Fourth after Pentecost	5. MORNING STAR CHORUS
Fifth after Pentecost	6. SILENT BIRTHQUAKES
Sixth after Pentecost	7. OCEAN STAMPEDE
Seventh after Pentecost	8. WHIRLWIND CLAY
Eighth after Pentecost	9. SUFFERING TREE
Ninth after Pentecost	10. EDEN SUNSET
Tenth after Pentecost	11. DESERT FOX
Eleventh after Pentecost	12. ENOCH ROCK
Twelfth after Pentecost	13. FLOOD BIRD
Thirteenth after Pentecost	14. RAINBOW BLAST
Fourteenth after Pentecost	15. SILLY SEED
Fifteenth after Pentecost	16. FLAME TREE
Sixteenth after Pentecost	17. FREEDOM BREAD
Seventeenth after Pentecost	18. TIDAL SWEEP
Eighteenth after Pentecost	19. MOUNTAIN MAGIC
Nineteenth after Pentecost	20. MOLTEN THUNDER
Twentieth after Pentecost	21. SUMMIT BANQUET
Twenty-first after Pentecost	22. MANNA MADNESS
Twenty-second after Pentecost	23. SNAKE DANCE
Twenty-third after Pentecost	24. FIRE VOICE
Twenty-fourth after Pentecost	25. EAGLE WINDS
Twenty-fifth after Pentecost	41. LION ANGER
Twenty-sixth after Pentecost	42. EARTH WAIL
Twenty-seventh after Pentecost	44. NEW HUMAN
Last Sunday after Pentecost	26. CANAAN DEW

A worship sequence using these Birthquake materials may begin with the Advent season or the Pentecost season. Because the number of Birthquake units is limited to the 52 weeks of the year, several themes appear twice in the liturgical sequence.